NEW ENGLAND MEMORIES

DENNIS STOCK

NEW ENGLAND MEMORIES

Introduction by
NOEL PERRIN

A Bulfinch Press Book
Little, Brown and Company
Boston • Toronto • London

My New England

A few years ago I left my Vermont farm for a week. I flew down to Boston in a little plane and then from Boston out to California in a big plane. I was going to a conference at that exurb-of-Los-Angeles branch of the University of California called Riverside. And never having been in southern California before, I had come a day early. I wanted to see the landscape.

As it turned out, the landscape made me nervous. There were plenty of individual elements I loved, such as the double rank of bottlebrush trees marching up the avenue at the main entrance to UC Riverside. But the countryside as a whole was too naked for my taste. All those bare, lion-colored hills and all that sweep of sky left me feeling exposed and vulnerable – a little bit like a mouse would feel (I imagine) if you put it out in the middle of a basketball court. A New England mouse, anyway.

The first evening I devoted to looking at the city of Riverside itself. It's a small city by California standards, but quite a big one by the standards of New England. It has – or had then – 180,000 inhabitants, which makes it more than twice as big as anything in Vermont, New Hampshire, *or* Maine. Riverside is also bigger than Providence, Rhode Island, or Hartford, Connecticut, each the metropolis as well as the capital of its state. It is smaller than Boston.

I was staying in a motel out by the university, and what I decided to do was to stroll downtown just before dark. Some stroll! In the first place, downtown proved to be elusive. I'm not entirely convinced Riverside has one, at least not in the eastern sense of a thronged center where building density is much greater than elsewhere, where you can't easily park, where things are *old*. In the second place, I remained tense. It was the same mouse-feeling I'd had out on the hills. Only this time the streets were the cause.

I was walking down a broad avenue, which naturally crossed side streets at regular intervals. Every time this happened, I went into a state of mild panic – that is, I panicked once a block.

Don't scorn me entirely. Those were formidable side streets I came to, like nothing I had ever seen before. Each had six traffic lanes and two parking lanes, for a total of eight. At home in Vermont not even the two interstate highways are that wide. I'm not sure the Connecticut River is.

I found I had to force myself to cross each of these mighty streets. After the first couple I no longer had any fear of being squashed out in the middle by some crazy California driver. California drivers proved not to be crazy, but quite gentle – the few I encountered. Traffic was extremely light that evening, and what there was moved softly. No one shot round a corner with squealing tires, or threatened me by speeding up slightly, as drivers sometimes do in Boston – and in West Lebanon, New Hampshire, for that matter, in front of the shopping malls.

My fear – I knew it at the time – was quite irrational. Simply, I felt too far from the nearest tree. Or, rather, this being a city, too far from the nearest doorway. *Much* further than I would have been in Boston, or Providence, or Torrington, Connecticut. Because even when I had gained the far side of a street, I was still a long way from shelter. Those immense streets were not bordered by comforting buildings. They were bordered by emptiness. Every Laundromat and photo shop had been set back by at least a hundred feet, and the intervening space was generally paved. I couldn't even have burrowed into the soil, had a helicopter come thumping down to catch an unwary visitor.

That trip taught me a lot about California, but it taught me even more about New England. Opposites may or may not attract; they certainly do clarify each other. And northern New England and southern California must be about as opposite as any two parts of the United States can get. Not that that means total opposition, certainly not in our homogenizing age. Both, after all, are American places. They have much in common. Teenagers in East Topsham, Vermont, listen to the same American Top Forty songs as teenagers in Redondo Beach, and (except all winter) they wear the same bright sneakers. They don't eat the same too-rapid food as often, but that's only because they have to go all the way into Barre to get it. Fast food is not available in Topsham. (Church suppers are.)

And so it goes through the whole spectrum, from theology to garbage collection. There are Hindu ashrams and Buddhist monasteries in New England as well as in Los Angeles. Compactor trucks in both places make the same unearthly whine as they swallow the same plastic. Even scenically the two regions share much, from identical telephone poles to interchangeable road signs to similar-looking storage buildings slapped together of cement blocks and then painted pale green. (Somehow I find them even uglier in New England than in California, probably because I have a clearer image in my mind of what a New England building ought to look like.)

But if there are many likenesses, there are even more oppositions. As I came back on the jumbo jet to Boston and then on the little plane to Vermont (nineteen passengers, no cabin attendants), I kept thinking about them. It seemed to me that I saw the true nature of New England more clearly than ever before.

Let me start with the landscape, then advance briefly to the people, and finally I'll say a cautious word about the soul of this region. Not all regions have souls, at least not living ones, but New England does.

The central truth about our landscape is that it's introverted. It's curled and coiled and full of turns and corners. Not open, not public; private and reserved. Most of the best views are little and hidden. It was only after I started doing contract mowing of hayfields around town that I got behind people's houses and saw vista after vista that you'd never guess were there from the public roads. We like secrets. And, yes, our roads. They are narrow, except for a few monsters curving around Boston and Hartford. You will see no roads at all in this book of New England photographs, because the great photographer whose book it is doesn't much care for either cars or roads. But if there were to be roads, the one I'd pick to be emblematic of the region would not be one of the thousands of little dirt roads to be found curling and coiling all over the six states, including Rhode Island. They are indeed emblematic, but perhaps more of the past than the future.

What I would pick would be Interstate 91, the stretch beginning at mile 112 in Vermont, going north and coming over the crest of the high ridge just beyond Wells River. That section doesn't look like an interstate at all. What you see in the valley below is a pastoral scene with what appear to be two separate two-lane roads running parallel, a couple of hundred yards apart. It is the only place in this country I know of where an interstate has been domesticated, and instead of cutting the land apart it stitches things together. And that is an emblem of how our human-made landscape, at its best, interacts with what was originally here. I greatly prefer it to big faces on Mount Rushmore, or the four- and six-lane concrete strips that press down so hard on the poor suffering but still beautiful meadowlands of northern New Jersey.

Let me take my own farm as an example of how the land is arranged. If you were to drive by it on the town road, you'd notice a fairly handsome old brick house, with a big red double barn attached to the western end. Across the road you'd see a few acres of cow pasture, fenced partly with barbed wire and partly with very handsome stone walls. (You'd better think them handsome. I've put in odd moments for ten years, rebuilding and extending them. I pry the stones out of the pasture with two crowbars and a tractor.)

That's all you'd see, but it's hardly all there is. Behind the house, completely invisible except to one set of neighbors across the valley, is my best hayfield – which is also the best kids' sledding. I almost lost a friend once who couldn't resist observing, every time he came, what a fine three-hole golf course that field would make.

Across the road there is a great deal more. Behind the field you see, three other fields curl around a high hill (and a pasture stretches up it). To walk from one field to the next – *this* with its pine-covered knoll where the cows like to hide when they are about to calve, *that* with its oak tree older than the place, and its cliff boundary – is like walking from one stage set to the next. Everything is so up and down, and so deeply wooded, where it isn't pasture, that my little ninety acres offers a dozen places to get lost. Even after twenty-five years I don't know every inch. It was only six years ago – nineteen years after I bought the place – that I stumbled on the fort. It's a giant rock that some glacier left: twenty feet long, fifteen wide, and a dozen high. Centuries ago frost split it lengthwise and then split one of the side pieces as well, so that there's a T-shaped passage right through the rock. A hundred-year-old yellow birch grows in that crevasse; dense pine woods surround the rock, and conceal it.

What caught my eye as I pushed past the last pine was the fortification. At some point long ago children rocked up each of the three entrances to about waist height, and at least one of those children really knew how to lay up stone. It is beautiful work. An average of one new person a year sees it. I have begun to worry that I am showing it off too much.

That rock is not the sacred place on my farm; the great oak marks that. But it may yet become sacred – in fact, the whole farm seems to be in the process. Four years ago I gave away the development rights (my neighbors had to vote in town meeting to approve this), so that there will never be any houses in those fields – or mini-golf courses, either.

There are sacred places on nearly every piece of land in town, except maybe in our one small commercial zone. And I would claim that the deepest truth about New England as a place is that, with the exception of some Indian reservations, it contains a higher proportion of sacred land than any other part of the United States. By "sacred" I obviously don't mean formally consecrated to a religious purpose – though there's a fair amount of that, too, around convents and monasteries in Massachusetts, not to mention around the lamasery thirty miles north of me. I simply mean land valued other than commercially – land for which the highest use (as developers and tax appraisers say) is not discovered by finding what will bring the biggest cash return but by finding what will make the land most beautiful, most productive, or most healthy, and sometimes all three together. And, yes, when I make that claim, I speak in full awareness of the million acres of the Adirondack Preserve in New York, and the Amish land in Pennsylvania, and all those Civil War battlefields in Virginia, and Yosemite, and . . .

I'll offer just one piece of evidence for my claim – but what a piece! Five years ago, when I was first looking for ways to protect my farm, I did some investigation of private land trusts: organizations dedicated to land preservation. There turned out to be somewhat under five hundred of them scattered across the United States.

Some states had one or two; some had none. Connecticut had eighty-two and Massachusetts sixty. No state outside New England came even close to those figures.

The people of New England are a good deal harder to generalize about than the land. We are a seacoast people and a lakeshore people as well as land-lovers. There are sacred coves, too. We may not have any seriously large cities except Boston, but we have hundreds of mill towns, some grimy, some not. We are partly French-Canadian, partly old Yankee, partly Italian, partly twenty other things. There are Mashpee Indians on Cape Cod and there is a jai alai fronton in Hartford. There is now one county in Vermont that has an actual majority of upscale newcomers, and in that county a term like "Sunday brunch" is heard more frequently than a term like "church supper." I believe they have hot tubs, too.

But climate and topography do play a role in determining human character, and furthermore, the example set by old New Englanders seems to have an effect. That same county also has an enormous number of houses heated by wood stoves, and the sale of chain saws to newcomers is brisk. Despite the enormous changes of the last twenty years, I think it is still accurate to say that the basic New England characteristic is a kind of humorous stoicism. You *expect* it to snow just before you have to drive a hundred miles, and you can assume it won't just when you have a day off to ski. You are not surprised when your pipes freeze, and you probably have a wry comment to make. I love one I heard about last fall, made by a woman in New Hampshire.

She herself lives in a small city, but she has a daughter in the country who runs a cider press. She had filled her car with apples at that press, to take to another daughter in town, who was going to make applesauce. Before she could deliver them, a storm came up, and blew over a fifty-foot tree in her yard, right on top of the apples. There are a good many things one might think to say at such a moment. "It sure put a cleat in my car," she said. "I guess I've got a convertible now." Sounds just like New England to me.

What is the soul of New England? Something inward, something a little cold even, at least that's how it's going to strike a newcomer. But something fiercely determined, and even more fiercely protective. Almost relishing discomfort. Able to endure almost any adversity and just get stronger. The one thing that may sicken it is too much ease and prosperity – which, indeed, I suspect is true for almost every region with a soul. Somewhat more tied to the past than any other part of America except a very little bit of the South.

And yet any living soul can change, and must. New ideas gather force in New England with some frequency. Once it was the idea that slavery should be abolished. Then the idea that everybody should be educated. Right now two ideas are strong. And hence two changes I have seen in my own conservative Vermont over the past twenty years are, first, a mighty tide of environmentalism and, second, a very rapid alteration in the relation between the sexes.

One of the events I missed during my week at Riverside was a barn raising on a new organic farm on the other side of town. When I got back, an aged neighbor (still able to use a hammer) was telling me about it. He had been there, helping. "You ain't going to believe this," he said gleefully. "They was twenty carpenters up on that roof – and damn near half of them was *wimmen!*"

There are barn raisings still to come in New England. New Englanders of every stripe will be up there, risking their necks, and preserving the sense of community that has kept us going for the past three hundred years.

Noel Perrin

PICTURES

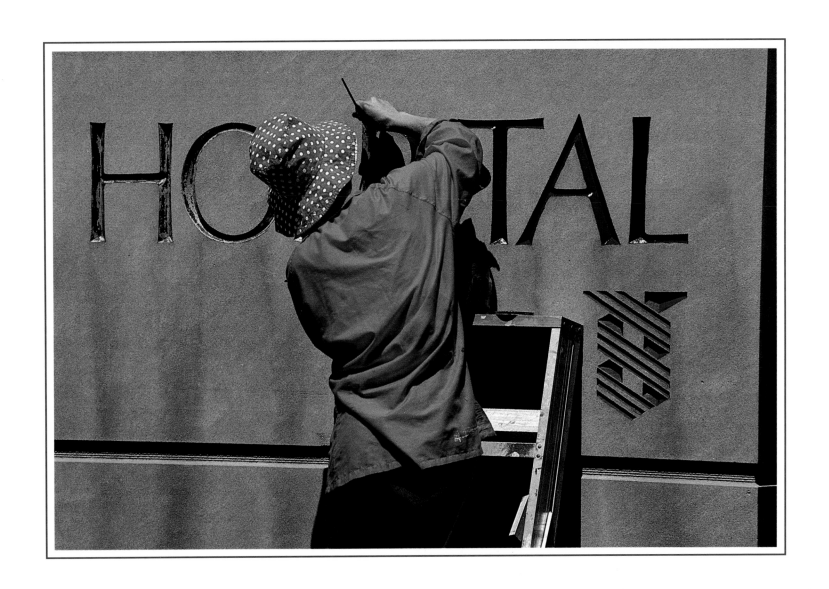

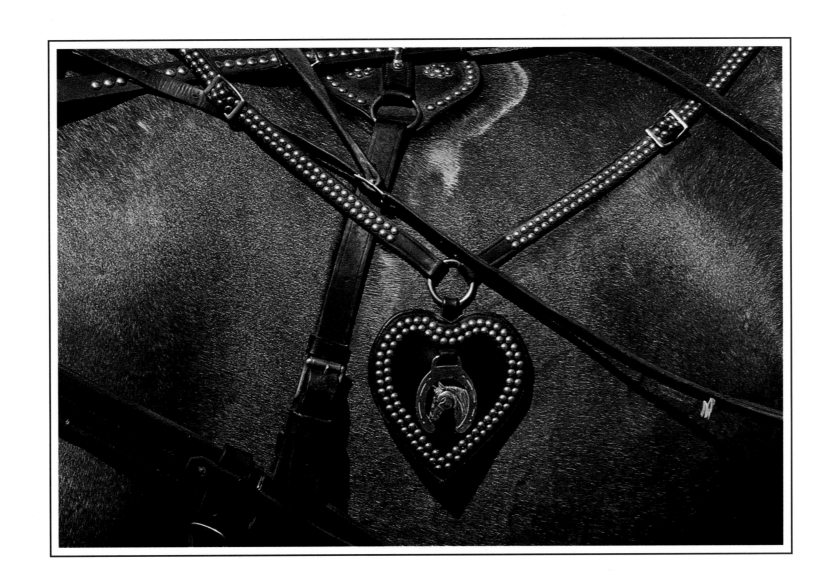

CATALOGUE

DUSK LIGHTS AN OLD WOODEN
STATION WAGON
OM4 Camera, Zuiko 50 mm,
f5.6-1/60 sec.

OLD GRANARY BURYING GROUND,
NORTH END, BOSTON
OM4 Camera, Zuiko 28-48 mm,
f8-1/125 sec.

COSTUMED WOMAN IN THE FIELDS
OF OLD STURBRIDGE VILLAGE,
MASSACHUSETTS
OM4 Camera, Zuiko 300 mm,
f6.3-1/500 sec.

STAINED GLASS WINDOWS OF
SOUTH STRATFORD CHURCH
IN VERMONT
OM4 Camera, Zuiko 75-150 mm,
f11-1/250 sec.

BARN SCENE AT OLD STURBRIDGE
OM4 Camera, Zuiko 75-150 mm,
f9-1/250 sec.

CHURCH ON THE GREEN
IN STRATFORD, VERMONT
OM3 Camera, Zuiko 28-48 mm,
f5.6-1/60 sec.

VETERAN'S CEMETARY IN LITCHFIELD,
CONNECTICUT
OM3 Camera, Zuiko 28-48 mm,
f11-1/250 sec.

AUTUMN FOLIAGE IN KENT,
CONNECTICUT
OM4 Camera, Zuiko 300 mm,
f12-1/125 sec.

REVOLUTIONARY WAR MEMORIAL
IN MANCHESTER, VERMONT
OM4 Camera, Zuiko 75-150 mm,
f8-1/125 sec.

TREE ISLAND IN BAXTER
STATE PARK, MAINE
OM4 Camera, Zuiko 75-150 mm,
f9-1/250 sec.

FIELD OF GOLDENROD
NEAR SEARSPORT, MAINE
OM4 Camera, Zuiko 28-48 mm,
f12-1/125 sec.

PORCH SCENE IN NEWPORT,
RHODE ISLAND
OM3 Camera, Zuiko 50 mm,
f9-1/250 sec.

DUTCH WINDMILL ON
CONANICUT ISLAND
IN RHODE ISLAND
OM4 Camera, Zuiko 28-48 mm,
f12-1/125 sec.

BEACH HOUSES AT YORK, MAINE
OM4 Camera, Zuiko 75-150 mm,
f16-1/30 sec., tripod.

SOUTH SHORE,
NANTUCKET ISLAND
OM4 Camera, Zuiko 75-150 mm,
f8-1/125 sec., polarizing filter.

BARN NEAR PITTSFIELD,
VERMONT
OM4 Camera, Zuiko 28-48 mm,
f12-1/125 sec.

BARN IN VICINITY OF KENT,
CONNECTICUT
OM4 Camera, Zuiko 75-150 mm,
f11-1/250 sec.

CORNFIELDS AT DANVILLE,
VERMONT
OM4 Camera, Zuiko 50 mm,
f6.3-1/250 sec., polarizing filter.

BARN MUSEUM IN NEW HAMPSHIRE
OM4 Camera, Zuiko 75-150 mm,
f9-1/250 sec.

CAPTAIN'S HOME IN NANTUCKET
OM4 Camera, Zuiko 75-150 mm,
f6.3-1/125 sec.

CASEY HORSE FARM IN
KINGSTON, RHODE ISLAND
OM3 Camera, Zuiko 75-150 mm,
f9-1/250 sec.

MAIN STREET, NANTUCKET
OM4 Camera, Zuiko 75-150 mm,
f6.3-1/125 sec.

DECAYING BARN IN GREENFIELD,
MASSACHUSETTS
OM4 Camera, Zuiko 75-150 mm,
f6.3-1/250 sec.

ENTRANCE TO HOME
IN MARBLEHEAD,
MASSACHUSETTS
OM4 Camera, Zuiko 28-48 mm,
f8-1/125 sec.

HOUSE FRONT OF
GINGERBREAD COTTAGE
AT OAK BLUFFS,
MARTHA'S VINEYARD
OM4 Camera, Zuiko 28-48 mm,
f5.6-1/60 sec.

HOUSE PAINTING AT
MARTHA'S VINEYARD
OM4 Camera, Zuiko 50 mm,
f8-1/125 sec.

REFURBISHING SIGN IN BOSTON
OM4 Camera, Zuiko 75-150 mm,
f9-1/250 sec.

CHESTNUT STREET IN SALEM,
MASSACHUSETTS
OM4 Camera, Zuiko 75-150 mm,
f6.3-1/125 sec.

MOUNT AUBURN CHAPEL WITH
BLOSSOMING DOGWOOD, CAMBRIDGE,
MASSACHUSETTS
OM3 Camera, Zuiko 75-150 mm,
f9-1/250 sec.

SPRING ON BEACON HILL,
BOSTON
OM4 Camera, Zuiko 75-150 mm,
f8-1/250 sec.

CROSSROADS IN SANDWICH,
NEW HAMPSHIRE
OM4 Camera, Zuiko 28-48 mm,
f9-1/250 sec.

BLOOMING APPLE GROVES
NEAR GRAFTON, MASSACHUSETTS
OM4 Camera, Zuiko 75-150 mm,
f9-1/250 sec.

LILY POND NEAR STONINGTON,
MAINE
OM4 Camera, Zuiko 28-48 mm,
f8-1/125 sec.

STREET SCENE
NEWPORT, RHODE ISLAND
OM4 Camera, Zuiko 50 mm,
f5.6-1/60 sec.

MARSHLANDS OF PLUM ISLAND,
MASSACHUSETTS
OM4 Camera, Zuiko 75-150 mm,
f4.5-1/60 sec.

CANADIAN GEESE AT REFUGE
ON PLUM ISLAND
OM4 Camera, Zuiko 300 mm,
f5.6-1/60 sec., tripod.

FOG RISING ON VERMONT LAKE
OM4 Camera, Zuiko 50 mm,
f4.5-1/60 sec.

TIDAL POOL AT
ACADIA NATIONAL PARK
IN MAINE
OM4 Camera, Zuiko 28-48 mm,
f9-1/250 sec.

COASTLINE AT ACADIA
OM3 Camera, Zuiko 18 mm,
f9-1/250 sec.

SHIP REPAIR YARD
IN GLOUCESTER,
MASSACHUSETTS
OM4 Camera, Zuiko 75-150 mm,
f8-1/250 sec.

SHIP PROPELLERS STACKED
AT SHIPYARD
OM4 Camera, Zuiko 75-150 mm,
f16-1/30 sec., tripod

HARBOR SCENE AT SCITUATE,
MASSACHUSETTS
OM3 Camera, Zuiko 300 mm,
f9-1/250 sec.

PEMAQUID LIGHTHOUSE
IN MAINE
OM4 Camera, Zuiko 50 mm,
f9-1/250 sec.

NEW HARBOR LOBSTER DOCKS
IN MAINE
OM4 Camera, Zuiko 28-48 mm,
f9-1/250 sec.

KITE FLYER ON PLUM ISLAND BEACH,
MASSACHUSETTS
OM4 Camera, Zuiko 50 mm,
f9-1/250 sec.

HIKERS IN THE
PLUM ISLAND ESTUARY
OM4 Camera, Zuiko 300 mm,
f6.3-1/500 sec.

CRANBERRY BOG NEAR PLYMOUTH,
MASSACHUSETTS
OM4 Camera, Zuiko 75-150 mm,
f6.3-1/500 sec.

MARTHA'S VINEYARD BEACH
OM3 Camera, Zuiko 28-48 mm,
f9-1/250 sec.

LOW TIDE AT ACADIA
OM4 Camera, Zuiko 75-150 mm,
f11-1/250 sec.

FISHNETS AT MENEMSHA,
MARTHA'S VINEYARD
OM4 Camera, Zuiko 28-48 mm,
f8-1/250 sec.

FISHERMAN'S SHED
OM4 Camera, Zuiko 50 mm,
f9-1/250 sec.

ACADIA COASTLINE
OM4 Camera, Zuiko 300 mm,
f6.3-1/500 sec.

NANTUCKET FERRY PASSENGERS
OM4 Camera, Zuiko 28-48 mm,
f11-1/250 sec.

CLOSED CONCESSIONS AT THE
BIG "E" FAIRGROUNDS
NEAR SPRINGFIELD,
MASSACHUSETTS
OM3 Camera, Zuiko 75-150 mm,
f11-1/250 sec.

AMUSEMENT RIDE AT THE BIG "E"
OM4 Camera, Zuiko 75-150 mm,
f8-1/500 sec.

MANASPEE INDIAN AT POWWOW
IN MASSACHUSETTS
OM4 Camera, Zuiko 500 mm, Mirror
f8-1/500 sec.

TOURIST
OM4 Camera, Zuiko 500 mm, Mirror
f8-1/500 sec.

WEIGHT-PULLING OXEN
OM4 Camera, Zuiko 75-150 mm,
f9-1/250 sec.

HOLSTEIN COW ON EXHIBITION
AT THE BIG "E"
OM4 Camera, Zuiko 28-48 mm,
f8-1/125 sec.

COWS WAITING FOR
LIVESTOCK COMPETITION
AT THE BIG "E"
OM4 Camera, Zuiko 50 mm,
f5.6-1/125 sec.

DECORATIVE HARNESS
ON HORSE AT THE FAIR
OM4 Camera, Zuiko 75-150 mm,
f9-1/250 sec.

EQUESTRIAN'S TENT WITH
DISPLAY OF AWARDS
OM4 Camera, Zuiko 50 mm,
f8-1/250 sec.

WEIGHT-PULLING HORSES
AT THE BIG "E" COMPETITION
OM4 Camera, Zuiko 75-150 mm,
f9-1/250 sec.

AUTUMN SCENE IN CONNECTICUT
OM3 Camera, Zuiko 50 mm,
f6.3-1/30 sec., tripod.

TURNING COLORS OF THE BRUSH
OM4 Camera, Zuiko 75-150 mm,
f8-1/250 sec.

THANKSGIVING DISPLAY
OM4 Camera, Zuiko 50 mm,
f5.6-1/60 sec.

PUMPKIN HARVESTING
IN THE BERKSHIRES
OM3 Camera, Zuiko 28-48 mm,
f9-1/250 sec.

SUNAPEE LAKE, NEW HAMPSHIRE
OM3 Camera, Zuiko 50 mm,
f5.6-1/250 sec.

FARMER'S MARKET
OM4 Camera, Zuiko 28-48 mm,
f6.3-1/125 sec.

TROUT FISHING IN NORTHERN
NEW HAMPSHIRE
OM4 Camera, Zuiko 75-150 mm,
f5.6-1/125 sec.

TURKEY FARM
OM4 Camera, Zuiko 50 mm,
f8-1/125 sec.

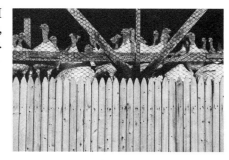

AUTUMN LEAVES
OM4 Camera, Zuiko 50 mm, Macro
f8-1/30 sec., tripod.

AUTUMN LEAVES
OM4 Camera, Zuiko 50 mm, Macro
f8-1/30 sec., tripod.

AUTUMN FOLIAGE IN
THE HILL COUNTRY
OF NORTHERN VERMONT
OM3 Camera, Zuiko 300 mm,
f8-1/125 sec., tripod.

CHURCH STEEPLE IN
PEACHAM, VERMONT
OM4 Camera, Zuiko 300 mm,
f12-1/125 sec., tripod.

SNOW-COVERED ICE FORMATIONS
OM4 Camera, Zuiko 50 mm,
f3.5-1/60 sec.

SNOW-COVERED HILLS
OF THE NORTHEAST KINGDOM
OF VERMONT
OM4 Camera, Zuiko 75-150 mm,
f11-1/250 sec.

ICE FISHERMAN ON LAKE CHAMPLAIN
OM4 Camera, Zuiko 300 mm,
f6.3-1/500 sec.

A DAY'S END FOR THE FISHERMEN
OM4 Camera, Zuiko 75-150 mm,
f6.3-1/250 sec.

CHRISTMAS WREATHS
ADORN THE DOORS
OF A CLASSIC NEW ENGLAND HOME
IN DEERFIELD, MASSACHUSETTS
OM4 Camera, Zuiko 28-48 mm,
f9-1/250 sec.

As in past books of mine, I hope that this book is viewed as if it were an exhibition, with very little concern by the viewer for titles, place, or time. My tendency when photographing is to free myself of labels and prejudices that would hinder me from pure discovery in form and color, be it in a rural or an urban setting.

While searching for sympathetic situations to photograph these many years, I have had to consider equipping myself with cameras and lenses that satisfy a variety of needs. When discovering a detail or a distant image, a broad system of sharp lenses and light cameras was essential to ease the burden of weight when traveling. For nearly fifteen years now the Olympus cameras and Zuiko lenses have served me well. Through these years as I exchanged OM1 for OM2 and presently for the fine standards of OM3 and OM4, satisfaction has remained intact.

My film is always Kodachrome 64 for its fine grain, fidelity to colors, and reasonable speed (ASA).

With usually two cameras hanging from my neck, I walk through the fields and villages, seeking the right perspective. My senses are fine-tuned, and the technical support systems are ready to facilitate my observations. Via the camera, I enjoy life a great deal.

Dennis Stock

ANTHOLOGIES
Let Us Begin, Ridge Press, 1961.
Creative America, Ridge Press, 1962.
America in Crisis, Holt, Rinehart and Winston, 1969.
Photography in the Twentieth Century, Horizon Press, 1967.
Photography in America, Random House, 1974.
Paris/Magnum, Aperture, 1981.
James Dean, St. Martin's Press, 1984.

DOCUMENTARY FILMS
"Efforts to Provoke" / United Artists.
"Quest" / Cinema Center / CBS.
"British Youth" / NBC.

Major magazine contributions include:
LIFE, LOOK, HOLIDAY, VENTURE, REALITIES, PARIS
MATCH, QUEEN, GEO, STERN and BUNTE.

Articles on Dennis Stock have appeared in:
ASAHI CAMERA (1956), CAMERA (1962, 1967, 1976), MO-
DERN PHOTOGRAPHY (1966), INFINITY (1967), APPLIED
PHOTOGRAPHY (1968), ZOOM (1972), NUOVA FOTOGRA-
FIA (1973), POPULAR PHOTOGRAPHY (1978), DOUBLE-
PAGE (1981, 1982), I GRANDI FOTOGRAFI / Fabbri (1982),
NEW YORK TIMES MAGAZINE (1984) and BRITISH PHO-
TOGRAPHY (1987).

He has also been the subject of a NATIONAL EDUCA-
TIONAL TELEVISION PROFILE (1958), and has been
featured in a program produced by NATIONAL ITALIAN
TELEVISION - RAI (1971).

MAJOR COLLECTIONS
Art Institute of Chicago.
Kunsthaus, Zurich.
International Center of Photography, New York.
Creative Center for Photography, University of Arizona.
George Eastman House, Rochester.
Musee d'Art Moderne, Paris.
Fotografiska Museet, Stockholm, Sweden.

AWARDS
First Prize, Life Young Photographers, 1951.
First Prize, International Photography, Poland, 1962.

ONE-MAN PHOTOGRAPHY EXHIBITIONS
Chicago Art Institute, 1963 (purchased for permanent collec-
tion).
Form Gallery, Zurich, 1966.
De Young Museum, San Francisco, 1970.
Traveling color exhibition on the theme of "The Sun," origi-
nating at Eastman House, Rochester, 1967-1974.
Woodstock Artist's Association, Woodstock, New York, 1973.
Sony Gallery, Tokyo, 1974.
Alpha Cubic Gallery, Tokyo, 1976.
Retrospective exhibition at the International Center of Photog-
raphy, New York, 1977.
Photofind Gallery, Woodstock, New York, 1985.
Urban Gallery, New York, 1987.

GROUP EXHIBITIONS
"Photography at Mid-Century," George Eastman House, 1959.
"The World as Seen by Magnum Photographers," traveling
exhibition, 1960.
"Man's Humanity to Man," Red Cross Centennial, Geneva,
1962.
"Photography in the Twentieth Century," traveling exhibition
prepared by the George Eastman House for the National Gal-
lery of Canada, 1967.
"Photography in America," Whitney Museum of American
Art, New York, 1974.
Arles Photography Festival, Arles, France, 1976 and 1977.
"Magnum Paris," Luxembourg Museum, Paris, 1982.
"Jazz et Photographie," Musee d'Art Moderne, Paris, 1983.

WORKSHOPS AND LECTURES
New York University.
International Center of Photography, New York.
New School for Social Research, New York.
Pratt Institute, New York.
State University of New York, Stony Brook.
Festival d'Arles, France.
Center for Photography, Woodstock, New York.

BIOGRAPHY
Born in New York City, 1928.
Apprenticed to Gjon Mili, 1947-1951.
Member of "Magnum Photos" since 1951.
Currently resides in Woodstock, New York.

AUTHORED PHOTOGRAPHY BOOKS
Portrait of a Young Man, James Dean, Kadokawa Shoten,
1956.
Plaisir du Jazz, La Guilde du Livre, 1959.
Jazz Welt, Hatje, 1959.
Jazz Street, Doubleday, 1960.
California Trip, Grossman, 1970.
The Alternative, Macmillan, 1970.
Living our Future: Francis of Assisi, Franciscan Herald, 1972.
Edge of Life: World of the Estuary, Sierra Club Books, 1972.
National Parks Centennial Portfolio, Sierra Club Books, 1972.
Brother Sun, Sierra Club Books, 1974.
California the Golden Coast, Viking Press, 1974.
Circle of Seasons, Viking Press, 1974.
A Haiku Journey, Kodansha International, 1974.
This Land of Europe, Kodansha International, 1976.
Voyage poétique à travers le Japon d'autre fois, Bibliothèque
des Arts, 1976.
Alaska, Harry Abrams Publishing, 1978.
James Dean Revisited, Viking/Penguin, 1978.
America Seen, Contrejour, 1980.
St. Francis in Assisi, Scala/Harper and Row, 1981.
Flower Show, Rizzoli/Magnus, 1986.
James Dean Revisited, Shirmer & Mosel, 1986, Chronicle
Books, 1987.
Provence Memories, New York Graphic Society/Magnus, 1988.
Hawaii, Harry Abrams Publishing, 1988.
New England Memories, Bulfinch Press/Magnus, 1989.

Printed and bound in Italy by Grafiche Lema - Maniago/Pordenone